Essential Care of Chameleons

Philippe de Vosjoli

Table of Contents

GENERAL INFORMATION

The goal of the *Essential Care* series is to provide hobbyists with the essential knowledge for raising and keeping amphibians and reptiles. For detailed information on breeding chameleons the reader should refer to other books and articles.

Chameleons

Chameleons are Old World lizards consisting of about 135 species in the family Chameleonidae. Half of all the chameleon species hail from the island of Madagascar. They range primarily throughout Africa with a few species found in the Middle East, Europe and Asia. The smallest chameleon is *Brookesia minima* from Madagascar, with an adult total length of an inch and a half, making it also one of the smallest lizards in the world. The largest chameleons are Oustalet's, Parson's and Meller's chameleons, all exceeding two feet in total length, with Oustalet's occasionally exceeding 30 inches, making it the longest chameleon in the world.

Some Characteristics of Chameleons

Eyes: Independently moving eyes that are mostly covered with skin are a feature of most chameleons (some brookesines have limited ability for independent eye-movement) but it is not unique to chameleons.

Digits: The most unique feature of chameleons is the fused prehensile digits forming pincer-like appendages. No other living lizards in the world have evolved this characteristic.

Casque: Casque is the French word for helmet and refers to the portion of the head defined by parietal and lateral crests in chameleons. The casque of chameleons evolved in part as a result of shifts in facial structure resulting from large eyes, the forward positioning of the eyes, and shortening of the snout and the muscles required for eye movement. Some species have evolved large casques that may serve one or more adaptive functions, such as a secondary sexual characteristic and possibly as a thermoregulator. A popular notion that in some species large casques may serve as condensation surfaces yielding a water source has yet to be confirmed.

Prehensile tail: Chameleons have a prehensile tail that provides them with stability when climbing in trees and shrubs, allowing them to anchor to surrounding branches and prevent falls.

Tongue: The other well-known feature of chameleons is their projectile tongue, which allows them to capture insects and other prey at a distance — up to more than twice the body length in certain species. The degree of specialization of the tongue apparatus is unique to chameleons but the use of the tongue to capture prey exists in other lizards.

Laterally flattened body: Most chameleons have laterally flattened bodies. This allows them to move more freely among tree branches and shrubs and to thermoregulate more effectively in arboreal environments.

Taxonomy

The taxonomic system proposed by Klaver and Bohme (1986), which emphasized hemipenis and lung morphologies is increasingly used by herpetologists and chameleophiles. Based on that system, the Chameleonidae are divided into two subfamilies. The subfamily Brookesinae includes members of the genera *Brookesia* (Madagascar) and *Rampholeon* (Africa). The subfamily Chameleoninae includes the Malagasy genera *Calumma* (e.g. Parson's chameleon, *Calumma parsonii*) and *Furcifer* (e.g. panther chameleon *Furcifer pardalis*) and the African genera *Bradypodion* (e.g Fischer's chameleon *Bradypodion fischeri*) and *Chamaeleo* (e.g the veiled chameleon, *Chamaeleo calyptratus*). The latter genus also includes the subgenus *Trioceros* (e.g. Jackson's chameleon *Chamaeleo (Trioceros) jacksonii.*
Klaver, C. and Bohme, W. 1986. Phylogeny and Classification of the

Tanzanian dwarf chameleon (*Chamaeleo rudis*). This neat little live-bearing chameleon is hardy as long as it is not kept at overly warm temperatures (maximum daytime temp 85 F (30 C). Mortality of babies can be high and it is suspected that this dwarf chameleon should only be supplemented lightly, no more than once a week to prevent hypervitaminosis.

Chamaeleonidae with Special Reference to Hemipenis Morphology. Bonner Zoologische Monographien 22. pp 1-64.

Chameleons and the Law

At the time of writing, all chameleons except members of the genera *Brookesia* and *Rampholeon* are listed under Appendix II of CITES, meaning that CITES permits will be required for transportation between countries. In addition, several countries also protect chameleon species. Wildlife regulatory agencies should be consulted before collection and import/export of any chameleon. In the United States, a number of states regulate the ownership of true chameleons. Hawaii prohibits the importation of chameleons. Other states such as Maine and Massachussets (these two states have some of the most peculiar herp laws in the nation) have permit requirements for the ownership chameleons, so check your state wildlife regulatory agency. For information on laws that regulate reptiles see Levell, J. P. *Reptiles and the Law*. Serpent's Tale. 1998. 612-470-5008.

Longevity

There are many generalizations about the longevity of chameleons, including that they are a generally short-lived species. In fact, as we find in other families of lizards, there is a wide range of life histories and life expectancies in chameleons. The following are some longevity records in captivity for some of the popular chameleon species:

Flap necked chameleon (*Chamaeleo dilepis*): 4 years

Veiled chameleon (*Chamaeleo calyptratus*): 8 years for a male and 5.5 years for a female, still living.

Fischer's chameleon (*Bradypodion fischeri*): 3 years from young adults and one still living. 4-5 years likely if raised from hatchlings.

Panther chameleon (*Furcifer pardalis*): Males, up to 9 years(*R. Carlson pers. comm.*); females, up to 5 years.

Carpet chameleon (*Furcifer lateralis*): 2.5 years in captivity; some claims of 3 years.

Parson's chameleon (*Calumma parsonii*): 8.5 years from large mature adults; 10 years or more likely if raised from hatchlings.

Jackson's chameleon (*Chamaeleo jacksonii*): Up to 9 years.

Brookesia stumpfi: 3 years.

Armored chameleon (*Brookesia perarmata*): We've had an anecdotal report of 3 years and several of 2 years from adults. Very likely this species has a potential longevity of 5 years.

SELECTION

Selection of Species and Sex

The first consideration before purchasing a chameleon is species selection. If you have no experience with chameleons then you first should develop your skills by keeping one of the popular captive-bred beginner species such as veiled and panther chameleons. Another consideration should be the climatic conditions of your area. If you live in a hot dry area, then cool-climate species that require a high relative humidity will be costly to set up and may not be the best choice. If you live in a cool and wet area, then heat-loving species that prefer a more moderate relative humidity may not be the best suited for your conditions.

The next consideration should be how much space you want to dedicate to keeping a chameleon. Any medium to large species of chameleon will take up a significant portion of a room if kept indoors under optimal conditions. You also need to decide whether a degree of responsiveness from your chameleon is important to you. Some species make better pets than others. Finally, as a general rule, males of many egg-laying chameleon species tend to be longer-lived in captivity than females. The best "pet" species for beginners are panther and veiled chameleons, particularly captive-bred male animals.

Selecting a potentially healthy chameleon

Based on visual inspection alone, there are limitations as to how effective you can be at selecting a potentially healthy chameleon.
As a general rule, you should NOT select the largest and most impressive chameleons, but rather half-grown or small specimens (very likely of a young age). Animals with a body length around three inches are a good choice for medium to larger species. These will generally be easier to maintain by inexperienced owners than babies.

As part of your selection process, you should then proceed with the following visual examination:

• Both eyes should appear of equal size and be open and active. They must not appear sunken.

• The body should have rounded smooth contours without the outlines of skeletal structures clearly visible.

• With imports, the outline of the hip-bones may be apparent. This may be due to lack of feeding while being held in a compound but it may also be a sign of disease or high parasite infection.

• The limbs and digits should appear even and without lumps or swellings.

Several species of chameleons are asocial and will not tolerate each other outside of the breeding season. This young flap-necked chameleon (*Chamaeleo dilepis*) was bitten by its cage mate on the head and the legs.

• The skin should be free of dry crusty patches and small nodules.

• Ask to have the animal climb on you. A healthy chameleon definitely gives the impression of a strong grip for its size, and it will tend to be active. Look at the vent area while it is climbing to make sure there are no caked feces or fecal smears. If present this could be a sign of parasites or gastrointestinal (GI) disease.

Captive-bred versus wild-caught

As a general rule, captive-bred chameleons are a better bet than wild-caught ones because they are less likely to be parasitized or stressed. If purchased as babies, you will also have a good estimate of their age. This is not an absolute rule and is not true for all species. For example, the great majority of captive–bred Jackson's chameleons are not successfully raised to maturity. In contrast, healthy imported subadult Jackson's chameleons tend to be hardy if their requirements are met. Captive-bred babies of the larger chameleons such as panther chameleons, are generally hardier than wild-caught adults if you know what you are doing and provide them with the proper conditions and diet. Obviously, if it is difficult for you to fill the dietary requirements of babies, then a young or subadult imported chameleon that initially appears healthy will be a better choice. Several species of chameleons, such as *C. montium*, which are tiny and delicate as babies, can be difficult to raise and maintain compared to healthy imported adults. The safest bet is to buy young and healthy-looking chameleons but not necessarily tiny hatchlings. The young hatchlings tend to be more delicate for the inexperienced and, for some species, are even difficult for experts to raise.

Number of animals per enclosure
Many chameleon species, including the popular veiled, panther, flap-necked and Oustalet's chameleons, are asocial outside of the breeding season and do best kept singly except for short introductions for breeding. As a general rule, males of most species should not be kept together in the same cage or, if kept loose, in the same room. Several species can be kept in sexual pairs or trios (one male with two females) if kept in large enclosures or indoor trees. We have successfully kept Fischer's, four horned, Jackson's, Parson's, carpet, Natal dwarf, Tanzanian dwarf and armored chameleons in pairs or trios. With some species we have noticed what appears to be social pair bonding of sorts (e.g. the animals always sleep next to each other). Mixing species is generally not recommended but we have seen combinations that worked. Close observation is always the best way to determine whether animals can be safely kept together or not and whether they will be stressed if kept under such conditions.

Jackson's chameleon (*Chamaeleo jacksonii*). Ever since Hawaii closed exports, this live-bearing species has become difficult to obtain. It is ideal for those living in cooler and more humid climates. Photo by David Northcott.

ACCLIMATION AND QUARANTINE

Acclimating wild-caught chameleons

Most chameleons that are imported are mature adults, which means that their potential longevity will be limited compared to an immature animal. In addition, many wild-caught animals are stressed, heavily parasitized and dehydrated. For any buyer they present a significant risk of loss within the first few weeks or months of captivity.

The general procedures for acclimation of imported chameleons are as follows: Set up the new animals individually. Offer water using a dripper two to three times a day to allow the animal to rehydrate. Offer food twice a day. Deparasitize imported chameleons with fenbendazole (Panacur®, Hoechst-Roussel) to remove nematodes. Tom Boyer DVM recommends four treatments at two week intervals. There are other regimens recommended, such as smaller doses given for five consecutive days. Other drugs for deparasitizing chameleons include ivermectin and metronidazole (Flagyl®). Consult a veterinarian experienced with chameleons for advice on anthelmintics and regimens best suited for your chameleons. For some animals, treatment with antibiotics may also be warranted if they show signs of listlessness or illness; an experienced veterinarian should be consulted.

Quarantine

If you already keep chameleons or other lizards, it will be critical that you quarantine new purchases in individual cages in a room completely separate from your other chameleons for at least 90 days. Meller's chameleons should always be kept in a room at a far distance from other chameleons, preferably in another building. Coccidiosis, cryptosporidiosis and fatal viral infections can decimate your collection if you do not apply methods that include quarantine with hygienic procedures. Coccidiosis has become increasingly common in veiled chameleons.

As a rule, quarantined acquisitions should be tended to AFTER the rest of your collection to minimize the spread of disease. You should wash your hands thoroughly with an antibacterial soap after caring for or handling newly acquired chameleons. Several chameleon experts know from direct experience the consequences of bringing in without quarantine that one beautiful and supposedly captive-raised panther, veiled or Jackson's chameleon. You have been warned.

During quarantine an animal should be closely observed for signs of illness including failure to eat or drink, listlessness, runny feces, worms, weight loss, gaping and forced exhalations, nodules on the skin, eye disorders and unusual swellings. Proper treatment should be provided and an experienced veterinarian consulted.

SEXING: VIVE LA DIFFERENCE!

How does one determine the sex of adult chameleons?
It's easy with most species if one looks for the external signs that might indicate whether an animal is a male or female. In many species the most obvious sign is that males have an elongated hemipenal bulge at the base of the tail, formed by the inverted hemipenes. In addition, because many chameleons are territorial they have secondary sexual characteristics that allow the sexes to recognize each other at a distance. Sexual dichromatism, differences in color and pattern between males and females, is one of the most widespread sexual characteristics in chameleons. For example male panther chameleons are typically brightly colored compared to the more drab females. On the other hand, female carpet chameleons are typically more brightly colored than males, particularly when gravid. Sexual dichromatism can also be temporary and may inform another of an individual's reproductive condition. A receptive female veiled chameleon has a specific color/pattern scheme while a non-receptive gravid female has another high contrast combination of color and pattern that clearly informs a male that she is not open to sexual advances.

Sexual dimorphism, differences in size and form between males and females, is another common secondary characteristic in chameleons. In many species such as panther, Oustalet's, and veiled chameleons, males are larger than females. Several complexes of chameleons have sexual dimorphism in the structure of the casque. High-casqued (*Chamaeleo hoehnelii*) and veiled chameleons (*Chamaeleo calyptratus*) are two of the best known examples in which males have a significantly larger casque than females. In others, the sexual dimorphism can include structures such as horns, rostral processes or dorsal and caudal crests. Jackson's chameleons for example, have large supraocular horns. Male Fischer's chameleons and Parson's chameleons have pronounced rostral processes. Male four-horned and crested chameleons have large dorsal and caudal crests. Some species of chameleons have minor sexual differences and can be difficult to sex such as Meller's chameleon and the armored chameleon. With other species, such as the spiny chameleon (*Furcifer verrucosus*), the sexes look so different that they appear as if they are altogether different species.

THE LIFE STAGES OF CHAMELEONS

Like most lizards, chameleons go through four broad life stages. Understanding these stages is important in the process of becoming a good herpetoculturist.

The four broad life stages can be categorized as follows:

I. Prebirth/embryonic;
II. Juvenile/subadult;
III. Sexually mature adult; and
IV. Old age.

Chameleon breeders are concerned with Stage I. (prebirth) because their management, such as nutrition of females and incubation conditions, impacts egg/embryonic development. Stage II. (juvenile) is characterized by initially small size and high body surface-to-volume ratio, followed by rapid growth and progressive decrease in the surface-to-volume ratio. The purpose of this stage is primarily to feed and grow. Intraspecies aggression and territorial behaviors are minimal, which means that with most species, chameleons at this stage can initially be kept together. However, in time larger animals will have a competitive advantage over smaller ones and end up intimidating them if they are kept together in close quarters. In several species of chameleons (e.g. flap-necked chameleons) there can be a subadult stage characterized by increased territorial and aggressive behaviors, but no breeding behaviors.

Nature's formula for most vertebrates is basically to grow an animal to a size where it can successfully reproduce, and then to divert energy resources toward reproduction rather than growth. This is what happens at stage III. (sexually mature adult), which is characterized by sexual maturity, sexual behaviors, territoriality, intraspecies aggressive/defensive displays, and aggression. Stage III (sexual maturity). adds the purpose of reproduction to a chameleon's life (sex was of no concern in stage II.). Once this stage is reached, growth rate is considerably reduced in lizards, particularly in females. In several species of chameleons, excess feeding and supplementation at this stage may lead to obese males and to females that produce unusually large numbers of eggs in the course of a year. For example, veiled chameleons in the wild will often lay only one clutch of eggs a year, with usually less than 26 eggs per clutch. In captivity, however, female veiled chameleons can lay up to four clutches a year, with 60 or more eggs per clutch. This is likely a direct result of feeding management and the enclosure temperatures maintained in captivity.

In many species of lizards, egg production declines after a couple of years. From preliminary research this also appears to be true with many chameleons. Stage IV., old age, is seldom reached by chameleons, but when it is attained, it may be characterized by infrequent or absent egg production, limited activity, reduced feeding and various subtle external signs of old age (e.g. scales more raised, skin more wrinkly). At this stage, cutting back on the amount of food and the caloric content of food may help extend life span.

Good herpetoculturists make adjustments in their feeding and environmental conditions to accommodate the requirements of each life stage.

Note : Life stages can also be divided into six categories as follows: I.) Prebirth/embryonic; II.) Hatchling/juvenile; III.) Subadult; IV.) Onset of sexual maturity/adolescence; V.) Sexual maturity; and VI.) Old age.

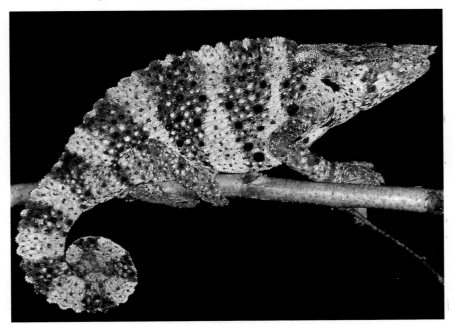

Meller's chameleon (*Chamaeleo melleri*). This is one of the largest of the chameleons. Unfortunately, imports can harbor viruses which can kill not only Meller's chameleons but other species housed in the same enclosure. This is a carnivorous species that will readily feed on smaller chameleons, other lizards and even small birds. Photo by David Northcott

HOUSING

A simple cage-less system for keeping larger chameleons
All adult medium to large chameleons, including *C. calyptratus, C. dilepis, B. fischeri C, melleri, C. pardalis, C parsonii* and *C. quadricornis*, can be kept free indoors on *Ficus benjamina* trees that are placed near windows receiving some sunlight a few hours a day. The potted trees should be placed in saucers. They should be lit with a spotlight on a photographic lamp stand, held by a clamp, or in a wall/ceiling fixture placed near the top branches of the tree. The light serves as a source of heat. Be very careful with placement of the bulbs so as to minimize the risk of fire. The lights should be positioned away from flammable materials such as drapes, and placed at least 12 inches from all branches and perches. The fixture should be firmly anchored so as not to fall. Ultraviolet (UV) radiation can be provided by hanging fluorescent fixtures with UV-B generating reptile bulbs. An economical alternative is to open a screened window (keep screen down and in place) when the weather is good to allow exposure to natural sunlight (optimal UV exposure will be between 10 AM and 2 PM).

Water can be provided by a drip bag hung in the tree. The water should be dripped through a tube and directed such that it drips onto leaves and flows toward the base of the pot. This method also waters the tree, and excess water collects in the saucer. Crickets which have had their hind legs pinched (preventing the prey

Indoor trees by windows with a spotlight and water dripper are ideal for keeping larger chameleons as long as one does not own cats or lizard-eating dogs. Children must be informed not to handle or pester chameleons when they are kept in this manner. Some of our best success with keeping chameleons has been achieved with this system (panther chameleon four years and still living and Parson's chameleon seven years and still living).

from escaping) and other prey items can be offered in a food container anchored in tree branches. Remember that a chameleon's tongue (except for Brookesines) will extend about one and a half times the body length, so feeding containers must have a depth significantly less than that distance to be effective.

There are a few other requirements for this system to work. The tree(s) must be kept in a closed room. When entering the room, do so carefully so that you don't accidentally strike a wandering chameleon with an opening door. Always look down, to make sure you do not accidentally step on and crush a chameleon. Also, there must not be cats or free roaming pets allowed in the room, although many dogs will learn to leave chameleons alone. In addition, the window must not be in a southern position such that it receives intense hot sun glaring all day long. This can overheat a room to such a degree that it could cause the death of a chameleon. Planting shade trees or shrubs outside a window to prevent prolonged intense sunlight is recommended. Think and evaluate what you are doing and monitor the setup regularly. Generally this has been one of the best systems for long-term keeping of larger chameleons indoors. Refer to *Notes on Popular Species* for temperature parameters.

Size of enclosures
An enclosure's size will not be a consideration with species kept on indoor trees placed in rooms. For other enclosures, general guidelines are that the perimeter of a cage [(length x 2) + (width x 2)] for larger chameleons be at least six times the total length (body + tail) of a chameleon. The height should be at least twice the total length of a chameleon. These are rough guidelines and variations are possible (e.g. less height but greater length). With smaller species and babies, enclosures equivalent to 20 or 30 gallon aquaria will work well. With smaller species and babies, larger enclosures are not necessarily better because the size permits ready dispersal of insect prey following introduction.

Screen cages
There are many specialists that advocate screen or wire mesh cages as the end-all of chameleon enclosures. Although screen cages are ideal for many species, herpetoculturists have successfully raised chameleons using a variety of methods. The greatest limitation of all-glass enclosures is size. Large all-glass enclosures are heavy and expensive. Most sizes sold in pet stores are generally too small to accommodate small trees and shrubs or to provide the height and space required by the more popular species. Thus, the great advantage of screen or welded wire cages with larger chameleons is that they are relatively light and economical for their size. They also usually offer the height necessary to include small trees or shrubs. Because the walls are screen or wire, chameleons will also be able to use the vertical surfaces for climbing and moving about. The "paw-at-the-sides" behavior sometimes performed by chameleons in too small glass tanks with

Another indoor tree setup. Some UV-B will get through glass panes but excess heat can be a problem in southwest windows. Opening a screened window during nice weather will allow exposure to unfiltered sunlight.

Welded wire walk-in aviaries are ideal for keeping chameleons outdoors in warmer climates or indoors if you have the space.

screen top enclosures will not usually be observed in screen enclosures. In general, the commercially available screen-sided enclosures are best for small to medium chameleons, although very large screen enclosures can be special ordered for large species. When possible, I recommend keeping the larger chameleons loose on indoor trees by windows or in large plastic-coated welded wire cages.

Glass enclosures with screen tops

Although some have made an issue of the suitability of glass-walled enclosures with screen tops for chameleons, this thinking is incorrect. Certain species require high relative humidity and do quite well in large all-glass/screen top enclosures. The reduced ventilation helps to maintain an optimal level of humidity. Generally the humidity-loving Cameroon species such as four-horned and montane chameleons do well in large (4-6 foot long) glass-sided, screen-top enclosures. Carpet chameleons will do well long term and have been bred and raised in glass-sided enclosures. Jackson's, veiled and panther chameleons have been successfully raised and kept long-term in larger glass-sided enclosures with screen tops. As could be expected, the small leaf-litter chameleons of the genera *Brookesia* and *Rampholeon* generally do well in glass-sided enclosures with screen tops. Many breeders initially raise baby chameleons in

There are now several kinds of screen cages available in the trade for raising chameleons. This is a Reptarium cage. A solid bottom of polystyrene foam was added for the placement of pots of *Ficus benjamina*. The cage contains a trio of four-horned chameleons. Three drip watering units were placed on top of the cage for watering. They are watered twice a day late morning and around 3 pm. The cage is placed in full sun only on days where the temperature is below 82 F. The ficus is large enough to provide plenty of shade. A bucket of soil was included for egg-laying. The four-horned chameleon is a hardy species that breeds well as long as temperatures are moderate and the relative humidity is 70-85%.

glass-sided vivaria. This reduces the escape of baby crickets and keeps them readily available for feeding. The reduced ventilation of glass enclosures is essential if you are raising high humidity species such as mountain chameleons. The often-mentioned stress of chameleons seeing their reflection in glass, I believe, is greatly exaggerated. This being said, the best enclosures for large chameleon species are large enclosures, no matter what they are made of. Keeping larger species loose on indoor trees in a room is even better.

Basking cages
Many people keep their chameleons loose or in screen cages indoors, but use a smaller portable screen cage to provide them with sunlight several times a week. To place a plant or tree in a screen-sided cage, cut a section of thick polystyrene board that will rest securely on the plastic floor frame. This will allow you to place a planted tree securely inside the cage and move it back and forth as needed without risking damage to the screen floor.
In addition to movable screen cages, I have walk-in aviaries made of welded wire in my backyard that I use to allow large species to bask.

Cats, raccoons, foxes and other predators
My first long-lived pair of Jackson's chameleons was mutilated and killed by a raccoon. They had fared well indoors and I had decided to put them in a welded wire cage outdoors. One evening, a raccoon seized their limbs through the sides of their cage and chewed them off. Any chameleon kept in large mesh cages outdoors may be a victim of this kind of mutilation. Other predators will also try to eat chameleons. Around the home, the greatest enemies of free-roaming lizards are cats which, both indoors and out, are lizard killers. Other predators to be concerned with are fox, skunks, and opossums, and occasionally the family dog.

A simple system for raising baby chameleons
For the first 4-8 weeks, baby chameleons of many species will fare well in 12 inch tall glass-sided enclosures with small leaved (standard *Ficus benjamina* and pothos are unsuitable) potted plants such as dwarf cultivars of *Ficus benjamina* or N*ematanthus*. The floor should be bare. A small incandescent bulb should be provided, to serve as a heat source and as a light for no more than a third of the enclosure. Also provide a full-spectrum or high UV-B fluorescent reptile bulb running the length of the enclosure. We have also had unusually good success raising baby veiled and panther chameleons using a small 50 watt halogen light placed on one side of an enclosure, within two inches of the screen top. These bulbs, even with the UV filter (do not remove them or you will burn your chameleons), apparently emit small amounts of UV-B. We've also had success using small, 35-50 watt halogen bulbs as the exclusive source of heat and light when raising babies of these species to a length of 12 inches, until transferring them to other caging.

For water, mist the leaves and sides of the enclosure lightly two to three times a day. Never spray water directly on babies. This stresses them and if sprayed at night can cause them to become too cold from evaporative cooling, risking respiratory infection (gaping, forced exhalation, blowing bubbles, puffy eyes). Food should be small crickets, seven to ten days old, depending on species (e.g. size) of chameleon, or fruit flies which have been supplemented. they should be offered twice a day. Once weekly, the babies should be transferred to an outdoor screen-sided basking cage with plants provided for shade. Babies will die quickly without shelter from the sun or if exposed to sunlight in glass or plastic enclosures.

Many hobbyists choose to raise babies in screen cages from start to finish, but this may not be the optimal rearing system for many species.

Substrates
For chameleons kept in large cages, the best substrate is simply newspaper. It is cheap and easily replaced as needed. With indoor trees, plastic sheeting placed under the potted plants will help to save floors. It can easily be washed and replaced. In outdoor cages the ground of most areas will be adequate as long as it consists mostly of soil. In glass-sided cages, either bare floors, newspaper or a fine moistened potting soil will work well. With most Brookesines, a moistened potting soil with a leaf litter cover will provide the conditions required. Avoid potting soils with perlite (white granules) which can be ingested accidentally.

Relative humidity
Lydekker, in his *Royal Natural History* published in 1896, had noted that the distribution of chameleons was in part determined by relative humidity. For chameleons in the wild, a primary effect of relative humidity occurs in the evening when temperatures drop, causing water droplets to form on surfaces such as leaves. This can provide a source of drinking water in the absence of rain. The other role of relative humidity is that it can reduce the rate of evaporative water loss that occurs during respiration. With the right relative humidity, the skin of chameleons will look and feel supple and velvety. In captivity, relative humidity should ideally range between 70 and 80% for most species. This can only be assessed with the use of a measuring device called a hygrometer. Inexpensive hygrometers (relative humidity gauges) are now available in the reptile trade and more expensive and accurate instruments can be bought from biological supply houses. Chameleon species from savannahs and arid climates can be kept at humidity levels between 60% and 70%. Many rainforest species will fare better at 75-85% humidity. As a rule, a relative humidity greater than 85% can lead to problems because both bacterial and fungal growth will be optimized, particularly if the high humidity is combined with heat. Good ventilation is essential if chameleons are kept at these high humidity levels.

If the relative humidity in a room is too low, a cool air humidifier or electronic humidifier will help raise the humidity. Always use clean water and regularly wash and disinfect the water container as instructed. A window or door (if chameleons are caged) should be partially opened so there is some ventilation when using a cool-air humidifier.

Ventilation
Most chameleons don't do well in saturated humidity or in rooms or enclosures without good air exchange. If kept in a glass enclosure, it should be relatively large. The entire top must consist of screening, and at least half the screen top needs to be left free of light fixtures.

Temperature and extra heat
Chameleons are ectotherms, meaning they depend on environmental temperatures to regulate their body temperatures. In nature there can be significant differences in temperature, depending on the ecology of a particular habitat. For example, during the day temperatures under the shade of foliage can be 10 or more degrees cooler than in the open sun. In weather extremes, underground burrows or shelters can provide protection from cold or heat. Environments with moisture and a breeze will cause evaporative cooling. In the wild, a chameleon can move between these different microclimates to maintain a desired body temperature. In captivity, conditions have to be provided so that a chameleon may warm up to its optimal body temperature and, once that temperature is reached, move to a more shaded and cooler area. For warm-adapted species such as panther, veiled and Oustalet's chameleons, this will mean providing a basking site where the area closest to a spotlight lamp that is safely accessible to the chameleon is around 90°F (32°C). For cooler adapted species such as Jackson's, Tanzanian dwarf, sailfin, four-horned and

Another example of an all-screen chameleon cage showing potted plants and, on the roof, a drip bag, and a feeding container..

Johnston's chameleons, the safely accessible basking site temperature should be around 84°F (29°C), with ambient or background temperatures in the 70's (22-25°C).

Failure to provide an area where a chameleon can reach its optimal temperature may be a significant factor in causing both metabolic bone disease and kidney disease, as well as causing a general weakening of the immune system, an inability to fight infection, and eventually, death.

Cooling

Several chameleon species such as Jackson's chameleon, Cameroon forest species such as *C. quadricornis* and *C. montium*, and a number of Malagasy chameleons will not tolerate high temperatures. If daytime temperatures are likely to exceed 85°F (30°C) (a temperature level which will already be stressful to some of these species) then a cooling system such as a window air-conditioner needs to be installed. In an emergency, under conditions of overheating, spraying animals with a cool water mist combined with a fan at low speed will help cool them down, but ultimately, in hot weather, air conditioning will be essential. In general, babies will be significantly less tolerant of heat stress than adults. Because air conditioners tend to dry the air and reduce relative humidity, a cool air humidifier may also have to be added to a room. In warmer climates, air conditioners or, in some areas, evaporative cooling systems will be essential for keeping cool climate species alive.

Nighttime

Under most conditions the usual nighttime routine is to turn off all lights. Chameleons appear to do best long term if there is a nighttime drop in temperature. Most species readily tolerate temperature drops into the low 70's (22-25°C) and even the upper 60's (19-21°C). For short periods of time, some montane species will tolerate nighttime temperatures in the 40's. A few will survive light frosts, though it is not recommended if avoidable.

Thermometers

There is only one way to correctly assess the temperature of a room or a basking site and that is to use a thermometer. Inexpensive stick-on thermometers are now available in the herp trade. Glass thermometers are available in hardware stores or drug stores. The preferred thermometers of serious hobbyists are digital readout electronic thermometers with an external probe for "outside" readings. By switching the thermometer to a probe/exterior reading and placing the probe in a warm spot of the vivarium you can get a continuous digital readout of the temperature.

Heating: Spotlights

Indoors, the best localized heat and light source for a chameleon is a spotlight. It should be placed in a reflector type fixture, ideally with a ceramic base. The inexpensive reflector type fixtures with a built in switch sold in many hardware stores will work for months, but eventually the switch will burn out and the fixture will have to be replaced. Ceramic base, reflector type fixtures with no switch (connect them to a surge suppressor with switch) or the more expensive photographic flood light fixtures with a switch on the cord will last many times longer. For cages, the reflectors can be placed upon the top, above screen or wire. Great care must be taken that the bulb makes no direct contact with the screen or wire. For indoor trees, nothing beats a photographic light stand and light fixture.

Great care must be taken when selecting the wattage of a light bulb, particularly for fixtures over relatively small tanks or cages. Too high a wattage will cook a chameleon in close confines. For small tanks, use 60 watt or lower wattage bulbs.

With all spotlight setups, great care must be given to placement and secure positioning of the fixture. Every year, there are fires started by poorly positioned or poorly anchored light fixtures. Pets can cause fixtures to tumble and a rug to start burning. Bad placement can cause a curtain to catch fire. In addition to placing a great deal of attention to the placement of spotlights, you should ALWAYS HAVE A SMOKE DETECTOR in rooms with heating devices used for reptiles such as spotlights. You have been warned!

UV-generating bulbs
When no sunlight is readily available, such as during winter months or when it is hazardous to provide sun in excessively hot or cold areas, UV-B generating reptile bulbs can allow for vitamin D3 synthesis. For the rearing of babies indoors, UV-B generating reptile bulbs are generally highly recommended. There is a great deal of confusion about the performance of various bulbs sold in the reptile market. For a long time Vita Lite®, which generates some UV-A and UV-B, was the only bulb on the market. The UV-B output is relatively low but if several bulbs are used and the animals can get to within six inches of the bulb, they can be effective. In recent years, several kinds of high UV-B reptile bulbs have appeared on the market. Examine closely any claims of UV output and effectiveness in vitamin D3 synthesis. To assure efficiency, full-spectrum and high UV-B reptile fluorescent reptile bulbs should be replaced every 6 to 8 months.

The best lighting: Sunlight What sunlight appears to do with many arboreal reptiles more effectively than just about anything else is allow them to raise their body temperature. Sunlight is nature's heat source. The other role that sunlight probably plays with many species of chameleons (there is limited experimental evidence) is to allow them to synthesize vitamin D3 which in turn will allow absorption of calcium, among other metabolic functions. This is what chameleon experts emphasize over and over, that chameleons require exposure to sunlight to synthesize vitamin D3. However all chameleons have not evolved identically, so there likely is a range of adaptation among the various species for fulfilling their vitamin D3 needs. Some appear better adapted to utilize dietary vitamin D3. Others need little exposure to sunlight to fulfill those requirements. The question is how much sunlight is really necessary? Based on what we know with humans, relatively little exposure to sunlight is probably all that is needed for vitamin D3 synthesis. For chameleons, exposing them to sunlight a couple of hours a week will very likely allow them to synthesize all the vitamin D3 they need. If exposed to sunlight for at least two hours a week, there will be no need for expensive UV-B generating bulbs. There are possibly other benefits to natural sunlight including psychological benefits related to light intensity and light quality. Some of the new "wide-spectrum" reptile bulbs may also provide some of those benefits. Much more species-specific research is needed in this area. Until we have more information, the wisest course is to expose chameleons to at least a few hours of sunlight weekly and/or to provide them with high UV-B reptile bulbs combined with spotlights.

Rules of sunlight exposure
The first rule is never to expose a chameleon to sunlight through glass. Instead, use screen or wire mesh. Besides filtering out much of the beneficial UV radiation, glass will create a greenhouse effect that will generate excessive heat which can rapidly kill your chameleon. However, in an outdoor screenhouse, placing a section of glass over a small area of the screen roofing or a screen side can be used to generate a warmer basking spot in cooler weather. In chameleon rooms, place the trees near screened (so the chameleon can't escape) windows that can be opened to let natural sunlight in. Be careful to monitor sunlit windows with southern exposure. If the windows are closed, a small room with southern exposure can overheat. The amount of sunlight entering a window can be regulated by panels of shade cloth or by outside plantings of select shrubs and trees.

The other general rule is to always provide a source of shade, preferably trees, when exposing chameleons to sunlight. For chameleons to thermoregulate, they must be able to move between a sunlit area and a cooler shaded area. Failure to provide shade has resulted in the deaths of many chameleons.

Chameleon trees
The best species of tree for keeping chameleons indoors is *Ficus benjamina*, a species readily available in supermarkets and nurseries. The standard variety is ideal for most medium to large chameleons. Small specimens of the small-leaved variety can be used to raise babies. These potted trees can be placed in a plant saucer to collect excess water. Dwarf umbrella plants have also been used successfully indoors, but the stems must be tilted or slightly bent because their vertical growth does not create good chameleon perching sites.

Outdoors, in warmer areas of the United States, *Ficus benjamina*, privet, mulberry, hibiscus and a number of fruit trees will work well with chameleons. For obvious reasons you should avoid tree species with spiny branches or very large leaves.

Because a wide range of chemicals are used in horticulture, it is a good idea to thoroughly mist the leaves of all newly-purchased plants with a hand sprayer containing a mix of water and liquid dish detergent. This must be followed by a thorough spraying/rinsing, using a sprayer head on a hose, to clean the foliage of pesticide residues.

Chameleon plants
Some keepers choose to use climbing plants creeping over branches as an alternative to indoor trees. Pothos is the best choice for this purpose, as it is hardy and grows quickly. For small species or rearing babies, certain *Nematanthus* species work well.

Wiedersheim's chameleon (*Chamaeleo wiedersheimi*). A very pretty species occasionally imported from Cameroon that is best kept in the upper 70's (24-27°C). during the day. Babies must be lightly supplemented, no more than once a week. Photo by David Northcott

FEEDING

Feeding schedule

Chameleons should be offered food daily, although a day can be skipped without any harm. During certain times of the year (e.g. summer for imported Tamatave panthers, winter for Parson's) some types of chameleons may refuse food of feed sporadically for extended periods of time. This is no cause for concern as long as the chameleon maintains good weight and seems generally alert and healthy.

Diet

Most chameleons feed primarily on insects although some will feed on snails, pill-bugs and spiders, and the larger species will feed on small vertebrates with a definite preference for other lizards.

Crickets (*Acheta domestica*) There is a myth in chameleon herpetoculture that crickets may not be a good staple diet for chameleons. I do not agree. Many chameleon species appear to do well with a diet of mostly crickets. The problems with crickets are usually the result of poor cricket husbandry rather than anything wrong with crickets per se as a dietary item.

Flap-necked chameleon (*Chamaeleo dilepis*) striking a cricket. Photo by David Northcott.

I know of Jackson's chameleons kept eight years on a mostly cricket diet and panther chameleons kept more than four years on a mostly cricket diet. We have a Parson's chameleon still living after nearly seven years on a mostly cricket diet. Crickets should be kept in clean well-ventilated containers that do not allow the growth of mold. They should be fed greens, grated vegetables and sliced fruit prior to being fed to chameleons. The risk of mold toxins such as aflatoxins accumulating in crickets fed on grain-based diets has been mentioned as a possible cause of liver disease and short life in chameleons. This should be considered a possible risk. Obviously, paying attention to the husbandry of crickets, including cleanliness, mold-free cricket containers, and sound, plant-based diets should help prevent this possibility.

King mealworms (*Zophobas morio*)

This oversized variation of a mealworm can be used as a small component of the diet of larger chameleons. As with crickets, they can be fed grated vegetables, apple slices and leafy greens for a few days prior to feeding. These worms tend to be fatty, so the quantities offered should be limited.

Wax worms and silkworms

Wax worms (*Galleria melonella*) are the caterpillars of the wax moth and can be purchased through mail-order. They can be offered in small quantities as a treat to medium and large chameleons. If fed to excess, particularly to small animals, they will be often be regurgitated.

Silkworms (*Bombyx mori*) are the caterpillars of the mulberry silk moth. In small sizes and in small numbers they are sometimes offered to vary the diet of chameleons. We have found them problematical causing constipation and possible impaction in some specimens. Many chameleons after initially feeding on them ravenously, later show signs of digestive distress and will refuse to feed on them again. We have talked to others who have experienced similar problems.

Roaches

Several species of roaches are available through biological supply houses and are raised by specialist chameleon keepers. Some states have laws controlling certain commercially raised species, so check your state laws before ordering (biological supply companies often know which states are restrictive). Roaches are generally very opportunistic in their diet, which means that their gut content can be altered by varying the foods offered to them. The most popular roaches that are cultured are Madagascan hissing cockroaches (not recommended except in smaller immature stages) and roaches in the genus *Blaberus*. In the nymph form, roaches are a good diet for chameleons but ideally should be tweezer-fed to reduce the risk of escape. We have one report of a Parson's chameleon choking to death because the hard spiny legs of an adult hissing cockroach caused it to become lodged in its throat and another report that suggests that the spiny legs may abrade the GI tract and lead to fatal infections. We don't recommend feeding adults of large roach species. Because roaches tend to burrow and hide, they are best offered off of forceps. Wingless forms and nymphs can be presented inside deep smooth-sided feeding containers. Roaches are not a good choice in vivaria with soil or bark substrates.

Flies

Many chameleons relish flies and they are a good supplemental food if gut-loaded prior to feeding. Only flies that are commercially raised and initially purchased as maggots to be pupated should be used. A special screen-sided fly-raising container is recommended; other pupation containers include deli cups covered with mesh held in place by rubber bands. The flies should be offered a high quality diet that can include powdered milk, fish flakes, baby cereal flakes, moistened cat or dog food. As with other insects, they should be fed a varied diet. Unless the nutritional content of flies is carefully controlled and evaluated, they should not be used as a primary diet. For transferring flies, a nylon stocking with the toe end clipped can be used to guide flies from a cage or jar into a chameleon cage. Taking advantage of the propensity of flies to be attracted to light will help you guide the flies into the enclosure. Ten minutes or so in a refrigerator slows fly responses long enough to allow transfer into chameleon enclosures.

Lizards and pink mice
It is quite probable that for larger species of chameleons, several vitamins including vitamin D3 will be obtained from the occasional ingestion of vertebrates, primarily other lizards. The giant chameleons may also feed on small birds or featherless nestling birds. I have observed panther chameleons feed on day geckos and Oustalet's chameleons in the wild feeding on panther chameleons. I have seen adult Meller's chameleons in captivity try to catch four horned chameleons and other smaller species to eat them. In captivity, green anoles as well as various geckos are readily taken by many of the large chameleons. Offering these large species a lizard or pink mouse every two to four weeks (not more often) will provide a wide range of vitamins and trace minerals along with calcium, protein of high biological value and essential fatty acids. With time, many chameleons will learn to take these from dishes. As a feeder lizard, several species of gecko are easily bred and could be considered as a food source (with apologies to gecko fans, who will be horrified at this suggestion). Vertebrates should make up only a small portion of diets for larger chameleons.

Escargots for herps
The gray edible snail (*Helix aspersa*), which is now farmed and has been introduced in a number of areas, can be a good addition to the diet of chameleon species that come from humid forests. Parson's, Jackson's and four horned chameleons are some of the species that will readily feed on active snails. The smaller snails, about dime size and with thin shells, are the best choice. Collected snails should be fed on mustard greens and soaked dry dog food for at least three days prior to feeding to clear out gut contents of possibly toxic plants. There is, however, always a risk of introducing parasites or toxins when feeding uncooked wild-collected snails, so controlled culture should be considered when possible. Snail shells contain much calcium, and the flesh is high in protein and low in fat and carbohydrates.

Plant Matter
At least one species, the veiled chameleon, will readily feed on plant matter when adult. Other species occasionally feed on plant matter and there are many reports of plant nibbling and incidental ingestion of plant matter while feeding on insects. With veiled chameleons, the first time they feed on plants will be noticed from the triangular bite marks visible on the more tender leaves of a *Ficus benjamina* tree. To increase the probability of a veiled chameleon feeding on plant matter, you need

A tame two year old male Oustalet's chameleon (*Furcifer oustaleti*) striking a king mealworm. This impressive species has been underrated by the herp community. *Courtesy of Reptile Haven and Chris Estep.*

to get it hungry. Offering crickets every other day instead of daily will often do the trick. Once a chameleon starts feeding on plant matter, you can regularly offer it chopped greens such as romaine and mustard greens, as well as green fruit sections such as kiwi and grapes. Certain flowers such as hibiscus may also be eaten. Be sure to remove uneaten plant matter daily because dried sections of plant matter if ingested can sometimes become stuck in the throat of a chameleon and cause it to choke. In time your veiled chameleon may eat a fair variety of plant matter, and 40% or more of the diet of an adult veiled chameleon may eventually consist of plant matter. The lower caloric content of a plant diet may help reduce reproductive rate and increase life span of this species in captivity.

Plants can be a component of the diet of all chameleons if one feeds them to food insects. Plant matter in the gut of insects may be a source of nutrients and thus benefit the health of chameleons.

Feeding babies
If you are expecting baby chameleons to be born in the near future, you should be prepared by making sure you have a source of small insects. Generally you can order baby (pinhead and one-week old) crickets by mail or special order through your pet store and have them within a week. For most hatchlings, week-old crickets will prove a good starter size. A good supplemental or backup diet are the large flightless fruit flies (*Drosophila hydei*) which can be ordered from ads in reptile and tropical fish magazines. For very small baby chameleons, smaller flight-

A clear deli cup showing crickets lightly coated with a vitamin/mineral supplement. A wire tie run through the side of the container will allow one to attach it to a tree or the side of a cage.

Veiled chameleon feeding from a tall plastic deli container. These inexpensive containers make feeding easy and are easily replaced as needed. They are tall enough to prevent roaches, mealworms and most crickets from readily escaping.

less fruit flies (*Drosophila melanogaster*) can be used to start them feeding. Fruit flies are easy to raise, but if you need a good supply, set them up in breeding containers several weeks before the expected births. The generation time of *D. melanogaster* is around two weeks and for *D. hydei* is about three to four weeks. Never offer a baby chameleon prey with a length greater than the length of its head. Baby chameleons can choke on oversized prey.

Vitamin/mineral supplementation

No area is more controversial and more vague in chameleon keeping than vitamin/mineral supplementation. What we do know is that extreme positions, either excessive supplementation or no supplementation, tend to be problematic. There is currently little research on the subject and commercial reptile vitamin/mineral supplements are not specifically formulated for the various species of chameleons.

The following is a general approach to supplementing larger chameleons which has proven successful and allowed lifespans of three or more years for several species kept primarily indoors. The formula is to combine one part finely ground calcium carbonate and/or calcium gluconate powder with two parts of a reptile powdered multi-vitamin/mineral supplement (not just a calcium/vitamin D3 supplement) that contains vitamin D3 and vitamin A.

At each feeding, the insect prey is dusted very lightly. This means for each adult animal, a small pinch of vitamin mix is added to a jar, the insects added and the jar gently swirled so the insects have a light dusting. The emphasis here is on a light dusting, not a heavy coating. Do not put large amounts of supplements into a jar so that insects are heavily coated with the product. This can lead to toxic intakes of vitamins and other nutrients, with resultant disease.

More Guidelines

Generally, a supplementation regimen needs to be adjusted according to feeding and husbandry methods and to species, a subject which by itself could fill a small book. Here are general guidelines:

1) For fast growing large species e.g. veiled and panther chameleons, supplement lightly one feeding daily

2) For medium species e.g. flap-necked chameleons and four horned chameleons, supplement 3-4 times a week.

3) For slow-growing and small species e.g. Tanzanian dwarf chameleons and Weidersheim's chameleons, supplement lightly once a week.

4) If your chameleon is regularly exposed to sunlight, use a vitamin/mineral supplement with vitamin D3 only once a week, dusting lightly. At other feedings use a vitamin/mineral supplement without vitamin D3.

5) For gravid females make a supplement mix consisting of two parts vitamin/mineral supplement and two parts calcium.

Some individuals only use calcium supplements and have had good results because they also gut-load their crickets with diets of a variety of foods that could supply essential vitamins and minerals. If using this approach, special attention should be given to offer a varied insect diet. Crickets should be offered a source of beta-carotene (e.g. cooked yam or grated carrots), vitamin C (e.g. orange slices) and the B vitamins (e.g. yeast flakes) as well as a feed that contains some vitamin D3 and formed vitamin A. Hobbyists using this method also expose their chameleons to sunlight. Miner-all® is a popular supplement for hobbyists in this category. This approach requires a measure of experience.

Food size selection
An easy way to determine an appropriate size of prey item is to select those prey with a length that is about the width of the head of the chameleon you are feeding. This is not an absolute rule. Occasionally a chameleon may eat a prey item, such as a lizard or mealworm, as long or longer than its head but the width of the head standard applies to dietary staples such as crickets.

How to offer food
In screen cages and glass-sided enclosures, the standard practice is to simply toss crickets into the cage or, for other insects, to place them in plastic deli cups or small food storage containers set within the enclosure. Chameleons kept in large walk-in cages or in indoor trees are fed by hand (if they are willing to do so) by holding out between one's fingers a prey item. Or they are fed by placing prey in larger food storage containers, deli cups or small buckets. This helps prevent escape of the insects.

Variety
There are many ideas about chameleon keeping which fall under the category of common sense but have not really been put to the test. One idea is that variety is necessary if one wants chameleons to live a long time in captivity. Another is that crickets by themselves are not enough to achieve good health and longevity. I have seen many chameleons raised primarily on crickets which achieved lifespans of three or more years, so I don't side with the radical "variety advocates". The situation is generally more complicated and can be summed up as follows. Crickets raised under healthy conditions and on a varied diet that also includes fresh greens, grated vegetables, sliced oranges and carrots, can provide a sound diet as well as dietary variety (through altered composition as well as gut contents) that will result in healthy, long-lived chameleons. If the diet can be also varied with other insects or, for large species, the occasional vertebrate, all the better. Don't let the lack of variety of insects prevent you from keeping chameleons.

WATERING

Chameleons recognize water by light reflecting against droplets from rain and dew or from moving water such as bubbles and wavelets of water dripping into a small pool. They generally are poor at recognizing still water although a few species such as the armored chameleons (*Brookesia perarmata*) will readily drink from a shallow water dish.

Drip systems
For most adult chameleons except for babies and the smallest species such as *Brookesia* and *Rampholeon*, a drip system should be the primary source of water provided. Several kinds of drip systems are currently available in the trade. A favorite are medical enteral feeding bags. Whatever system you use, adjust the drip so that the rate of fall is one drop per one to two seconds. The end of the drip tube should be placed in an area easily accessible to the chameleon. These lizards will readily learn to drink from the end of the tube. As with all watering systems in which container and outlet are used long term, cleaning and disinfecting with a 5% bleach solution must be done every two weeks. Drip systems should ideally be replaced every few months to maintain high hygiene levels.

Drip containers
Deli cups with a hole punched in their bottom or containers drilled to accommodate an aquarium air valve (sealed in place using silicone sealer) can be used as drippers. The problem with drippers is that water will fall from the container to the leaves below from which a chameleon will have to lick the droplets. To be effective, a dripper must be carefully positioned in such a way that droplets will fall and form on leaves. These drippers work well in heavily planted setups but in general a tube outlet will be more effective at keeping your chameleon hydrated. As with other drip systems, a water-collecting container should be placed on the floor of the enclosure and emptied daily.

Misters
In outdoor enclosures or indoor enclosures with drains, misters connected to a plumbing system and set on timers are an excellent way to water chameleons. Misters should directed toward easily accessible areas of foliage.

Rodent water bottles
Sipper bottles used for watering rodents are ideal for hand-watering chameleons. The chameleons are attracted not only to water droplets squeezed out of the ball tip but also to the reflection against the metallic tip. Putting the ball tip near or just above the tip of the snout and gently squeezing out a few drops is recommended as a secondary watering method to assure that larger chameleons are getting enough water. My wife will often use a drip system early in the day and a rodent bottle for the second watering of the day. When initially presented with

Hand watering a panther chameleon using a rodent drinking bottle. This is a good way to assure that larger chameleons get enough water. They are attracted to the shine of the ball tip as well as the dripping water.

A clear deli cup drip. A small hole is poked through the bottom using a fine nail. Only offer a high quality drinking water.

the tip of a water bottle, a chameleon may initially shy away. This should not be interpreted as meaning that a chameleon is not thirsty. Stay in place and continue dripping for several minutes and a chameleon will often come back to drink once it has determined that the system is safe.

Hand Sprayers
Hand sprayers can be also be used to mist the leaves and this is the primary method for watering baby chameleons. Remember that babies should never be sprayed directly, Instead, the surrounding foliage and enclosure sides are misted. For large chameleons, spraying lightly and gently at the edges of the mouth (do not spray eyes) will often elicit drinking behavior. Once started, gentle spraying as the chameleon opens its mouth will allow you to offer water to a chameleon. As with rodent water bottles, this is a good secondary watering method.

Pump sprayers
When you have a lot of enclosures or animals to mist or spray, a pump sprayer will greatly facilitate the process and prevent your hand from getting tired. Because algal or bacterial scum will tend to build in the water holding tank, it should be washed with an antibacterial soap and disinfected with 5% bleach solution monthly or more frequently. It should be thoroughly rinsed before use.

Water containers
At least *Brookesia perarmata* will drink out of shallow containers of still water. I offer a shallow water dish to all *Brookesia* and *Rampholeon*. The container, such as a jar lid, should have no more than a quarter-inch of water.

For babies, use a hand sprayer, adjusting the nozzle so it sprays a fine mist. On screen cages the mist will form small droplets from which babies will drink. Only offer a high quality drinking water.

BREEDING

As mentioned in the introduction, the emphasis of this book is husbandry. Breeding is too complex a subject to be covered in a booklet this size and the reader should refer to other AVS books. The following is a brief overview of breeding chameleons in captivity.

Most chameleons are egg-laying but a significant number of African species are live-bearing (several of the *Bradypodion* and some members of the subgenus *Trioceros*). Most chameleons are sexually mature by 12 months of age. A few, such as Parson's chameleons, may take longer to mature. In captivity some of the popular species, such as veiled and panther chameleons, may become sexually mature as early as five months of age. The carpet chameleon can reach sexual maturity at three months of age. The health consequences of reaching sexual maturity are relatively minor for males but can be of great consequence to females who must expend a great deal of energy and nutrients in egg production.

In captivity, heavy feeding and high levels of supplementation can result in females of veiled and panther chameleons producing abnormally large numbers of eggs with abnormally high frequency, shortening their life spans and increasing the risk of egg-binding and other

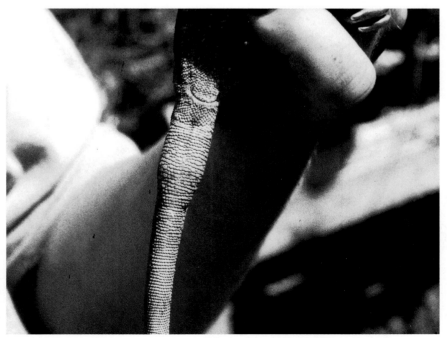

The hemipenal bulge is clearly visible in this male panther chameleon.

complications. Calcium stores can be taxed as large numbers of eggs are produced frequently, with a calcium crash (acute hypocalcemia) occurring after eggs pass through the shell gland. Calcium deficiency, whether chronic or acute, with or without hypocalcemia, is commonly associated with failure to lay and egg-binding. Thus, quality of diet, frequency of feeding, and rates of supplementation affect reproductive success in some species.

Eggs of panther chameleon carefully unburied from under the base of a ficus.

How to breed chameleons

The first step in breeding chameleons is to have at least one healthy male and female. Do not attempt to breed weak, thin or sick animals. Some chameleons breed best when allowed a period of rest (brumation). In the United States, many species will rest (they won't feed as usual and won't breed) during late fall to early spring. Some species can breed year-round as long as extended daylight, optimal temperatures and food are available. Some chameleons can be kept in pairs year-round (e.g. four-horned and Fischer's chameleons). Others are best kept separately except for breeding (e.g. panther and veiled chameleons). A few species can be kept in groups.

Most chameleons breed easily. Basically, if females are receptive, breeding will usually occur soon after a male is introduced into the female's enclosure. A non-receptive female will quickly let a male know that she is not in a receptive mood/state. The male should be removed within 24 hours if this is the case, with another introduction tried again later. The females of several species of egg-laying chameleons, such as panther, veiled and Oustalet's chameleons, will adopt a gravid/nonreceptive coloration after a successful breeding.

Following copulation, the gestation period of many egg-laying species is about a month, but because females can store sperm it is not always possible to accurately determine the time-course of fertilization to egg-laying or the birth of live young. Determining a stage of the reproductive cycle in a female is not always easy. Generally, females will appear plump and swollen when they ovulate. In egg-layers, after fertilization and after the eggs pass through the shell gland, the outline of individual eggs will become visible in many species. Individual eggs can also be palpated through the abdominal wall at this time. This is a good time to make available to the female an accessible container with at least 8 to 24 inches (depending on species) of compacted moist sandy soil in large plastic storage container. A small potted ficus should be placed on top of the soil because most female chameleons prefer to lay their eggs at the base of trees or shrubs. The root ball provides a source of moisture and some insulation. As the babies hatch they can quickly climb up the tree or shrub and hide from potential predators. Failure to provide the proper egg-laying site can contribute to the risk of egg-binding. After egg-laying, the female is provided with water and food. The eggs are carefully dug up and placed in an incubation container.

Incubation
The incubation of eggs in chameleons tends to fall in three general categories:

1) Those that should be incubated at 68-74°F (20-23°C) with an ideal of about 72°F (22°C). This includes many montane and forest species such as Johnston's, four-horned, and Parson's chameleons.
2) Those that can be incubated at 76-84°F (24-29°C), such as panther, veiled, flap-necked and Oustalet's chameleons.
3) Eggs that may require a diapause or rest period in their incubation. For some species of chameleons from areas with extended dry and/or cool seasons it is hypothesized that a cool period preceding normal warm incubation temperatures may be a prerequisite for triggering or speeding up development. This has been hypothesized for species like the common chameleon (*Chamaeleo chamaeleon*).

Eggs of chameleons from cool moist areas are best incubated in moistened vermiculite. Eggs of chameleons from drier areas have been incubated successfully in vermiculite, vermiculite/perlite mixes, or pure perlite. A layer of incubating medium about 1.5 inches deep is placed in an incubating container such as a plastic food storage container, deli cup or incubator base. The container needs a few small air holes. The eggs are buried on their sides leaving about one third exposed to allow monitoring. Depending on species and incubation conditions, incubation may last from as little as 45 days (some *Brookesia*) to as long as two years (Parson's chameleon). Consult other books for more details on this subject.

NOTES ON POPULAR SPECIES

PANTHER CHAMELEON (*Furcifer pardalis*)
Origin/Distribution: Widespread in northern Madagascar.
Size: Males up to 20 inches (51 cm) .
Sexing: Males are much larger than females. They have a well defined white lateral line running the length of the body. They are more colorful. They have hemipenal bulges.
Longevity: From one to five years for females. From two to seven years for males.
Acclimation: Many imports are parasitized with filarial worms. For this reason the smaller and younger the animal, the better the chance of having a chameleon with little or no filarial worm infestation and one that will have a long life. Imports may be infected with nematodes and other internal parasites.
Care: Indoors, the best way to keep adults is on *Ficus benjamina* trees in front of screened windows. A spotlight on a photographic light tripod is the best way to provide heat.
Temperature: Daytime background 76-82°F (24-27°C). Basking site 90°F (32°C). Nighttime 60-76°F (16-24°C). Food insects can be offered by hand or in feeding containers. The general principles in this book will apply.

CARPET CHAMELEON (*Furcifer lateralis*)
Origin: Madagascar.
Size: 6-7 inches (15-18 cm) total length for males.
Sexing: Males slightly larger than females. Males more green, more slender-bodied and with visible hemipenal bulges.
Longevity: Short-lived in the wild, but can live up to two to three years in captivity if raised from hatchling.
Selection: If buying imports, always pick the smallest animals. When available, captive-bred baby carpet chameleons are the best choice for starting with this species. Captive-bred specimens tend to be hardy, grow fast and will generally fare well.
Care: The commonly imported small form of the carpet chameleon is usually collected around the capital of Madagascar, Tananarivo, located in the central highlands. This form does best if kept cooler, in the upper 70's, during the day with 85°F (30°C) the upper limit of tolerance (use only at the basking site). Temperatures can drop into the 60's at night. The large form, "major", is collected from the hot west coast and does better at warmer temperatures, low to mid 80's, as background, with a basking site up to 90°F (32°C). Carpet chameleons fare well as single pairs in either screen or large glass-sided with screen top enclosures. My experience with this species is that it does better in large, well-designed all-glass vivaria with screen top, full spectrum bulbs and spotlight. one to two hours of sunlight weekly is beneficial. A sandy soil over a drainage layer planted with small trees or shrubs works well outdoors.

FLAP NECKED CHAMELEON *(Chamaeleo dilepis)*
Six or seven subspecies are recognized.
Size: Depending on subspecies and population, size can vary between 9 and 14 inches. The larger forms are quite impressive and surprising to those who have never seen such large chameleons.
Sexing: In most but not all subspecies, males can be recognized by the presence of small tarsal spurs. In general the body build of males is more slender. Males also have hemipenal bulges and the interstitial skin of the throat in many of the forms is a vivid orange.
Acclimation: As for all chameleons, flap-necks should be deparasitized for nematodes using fenbendazole (Panacur®). Our personal experience with this species is that it is quite hardy and often does well. At the time of writing we have a female that was obtained as a large adult and has been in our collection for over 20 months. We have captive-hatched babies that are now ten months old.
Care: Standard chameleon care, similar to that of *C. pardalis.*

FISCHER'S CHAMELEON *(Bradypodion fischeri)*
This is a generally hardy species that deserves much more effort to establish in captivity. I rank it as one of the hardier chameleon species, particularly the smaller *B. fischeri tavetanus.* There are six subspecies.
Origin: Kenya and Tanzania. Three subspecies of Fischer's chameleons are commonly imported from Tanzania, the large *B. f. fischeri* that can reach a total length of 15 inches (38 cm), the mid-size *B. f. multituberculatus* and the small *B. f. tavetanus.*
Longevity: We have kept this species for three years from imported adults.
Sexing: In all but one subspecies the males have large rostral processes. Males are also more slender bodied, have hemipenal bulges and have distinctive color and pattern.
Acclimation: Some imports arrive healthy, whereas others have signs of internal parasites and should be treated accordingly.
Care: Fischer's chameleon prefer temperatures in the mid to high 70's (25-27°C)and will tolerate temperatures up to the low 80's (27-29°C). Basking site temperature 82-85°F (28-30°C). Nighttime temperatures can safely drop into the 60's (15-18°C). The small subspecies can readily be kept in pairs, even in relatively small cages. The larger subspecies can be kept in pairs in large cages.

FOUR-HORNED CHAMELEON *(Chamaeleo quadricornis)*
Origin of imported animals: Cameroon
Sexing: Males grow larger and have distinctive snout horns and large dorsal and caudal crests.
Care: This hardy species does best if kept at moderate temperatures in the mid to upper 70's but will tolerate temperatures in the low 80's. Basking site temperature 85°F (30°C). Night temperatures can safely drop into the 60's. Relative humidity of 70-80% is a requirement. Water twice a day. Offer weekly exposure to sunlight or keep under high UV-B reptile bulbs. Plenty of shade should always be provided. Can be kept in pairs or trios in large cages or indoor trees.

A male panther chameleon (*Furcifer pardalis*) is probably the best choice for a first time chameleon owner. If possible start with a young captive-bred individual. In this species, males are larger and more colorful than females.

Male Fischer's chameleon (*Bradypodion fischeri*). This hardy species is currently imported with some regularity from Tanzania. Although it breeds readily, relatively few hobbyists have successfully incubated the eggs full term. Photo by David Northcott.

A free roaming Moroantsetra male panther chameleon in a pet store.

Male panther chameleon from the area of Ambanja. *Photo by Liddy Kammer.*

Note: Sailfin chameleons (*Chamaeleo montium*) can generally be kept in the same manner but are less hardy and more heat sensitive.

JACKSON'S CHAMELEON (*Chamaeleo jacksonii*)
Origin: East Africa but most U.S. animals originate from Hawaii where the subspecies *xantholophus* was introduced.
Sexing: Males have three large horns. They are less heavily bodied than females.
Size: Up to 13 inches (32 cm)
Care: Keep in screen or welded wire cages or indoor trees. Temperatures of 76-82° (25-28°C) will be suitable during the day and can drop safely into the 50's and 60's at night. A basking light is recommended for thermoregulation, with a basking site temperature of about 85°F (30°C). Regular exposure to a UV-B source, preferably sunlight, is recommended. Relative humidity should be 70-80% with good ventilation. Will feed on insects but will also readily take small snails. Large specimens can be offered pink mice up to twice a month as a source of additional nutrients. Can be kept in pairs in walk-in cages, otherwise best kept singly. This species loves to eat flies.

OUSTALET'S CHAMELEON (*Furcifer oustaleti*)
Origin: Madagascar, wide distribution.
Size: Oustalet's chameleons are one of the three largest chameleons as well as the longest chameleon, with males from Morondava said to occasionally exceed 30 inches (76 cm). Like panthers, there are several geographical forms that can vary significantly in their husbandry requirements. All imports tend to be heavily parasitized and must be treated, at least with fenbendazole (Panacur®) for up to four treatments. Mortality in adult imports within the first year tends to be high. When available, babies are an excellent choice for starting with this impressive species.
Sexing: Males are larger, exhibit hemipenal bulges, have a larger casque and distinctive coloration. Females are smaller, heavier bodied and usually green. They will have a high contrast red pattern when gravid.
Care: Oustalet's that are sympatric with panther chameleons (northern parts of their range) should be kept like panther chameleons. The large western form (larger with high contrast black and white casque) is adapted to more arid environments and will require background temperatures in the 80's (27-31°C) (and a 90-95°F (32-35°C) basking temperature to fare well.
Diet: In addition to insects, this species when adult likes lizards and I believe these prey can play an important part in providing the chameleons with the proper nutrients. I have personally observed a large male Oustalet's eating a subadult panther chameleon in the wild. This species relishes geckos.

MELLER'S CHAMELEON (*Chamaeleo melleri*)
Meller's chameleon is an awesome beast and one of the largest of the chameleons. It is also notorious for having a high mortality rate and

can carry one or more viruses that can decimate a chameleon collection. In general the best course for success with this species is to start with captive-hatched juveniles. Meller's must be segregated from other chameleons. They will try to eat smaller species and attack larger ones, with a single bite carrying a significant risk of infecting an animal with a fatal virus. Only for experienced keepers.

Sexing: No obvious external signs. The one male I dissected appeared larger and heavier-bodied than females.

Care: Can be kept like panther chameleons, either on indoor trees or in large cages.

Diet: This is the most aggressively carnivorous of the chameleons, particularly relishing other lizards including other chameleons.

TANZANIAN DWARF CHAMELEON *(Chamaeleo rudis)*

To date there have been few efforts to establish this species in captivity although it has many features which make it an ideal chameleon. It is attractive, small, live-bearing and reasonably hardy.

Origin: There are four subspecies. Imports currently originate from Tanzania.

Size: 6 inches (15 cm) total length.

Sexing: Females are uniform green, heavy-bodied and lack hemipenal bulges. Males have hemipenal bulges, more slender body and distinctive coloration.

Care: Generally daytime/background temperatures in the mid to high 70's suit it well. It enjoys temperatures in the low 80's but will be stressed above 85°F (30°C). Weekly exposure to sunlight is recommended. Does well at a relative humidity of 60-70%. Males should be kept separately but pairs or trios (a male and two females) can be kept together in large cages. Babies may be difficult to raise but it is suspected that over-supplementation may be a cause. Supplement lightly once a week and expose to a UV source. Sexual maturity is reached by ten months. Besides crickets, it relishes flies. A common cause of death is overheating.

VEILED CHAMELEON *(Chamaeleo calyptratus)*

Distribution: Yemen/Saudi Arabia border.

Size: up to 24 inches (61 cm) total length.

Sexing: Males are larger, with a larger casque and hemipenal bulges.

This is the only chameleon firmly established in herpetoculture, with at least tenth generation breeding.

There are two recognized subspecies: *C. c. calyptratus*, which is the most common in herpetoculture and *C. c. calcarifer* which has a smaller casque.

Some veileds display several of the best qualities of chameleon, while others rank as some of the most wary and aggressive of the lot. If you want a pet, raise a veiled chameleon in an environment with human activity, such as in a kitchen, and interact with it frequently, starting when it has a body length of about two inches. This means taking the time for two or three short (5-10 minutes) sessions to get it to climb on a finger, hand-feed, permit its carrying, and climb from hand to hand.

As it gets larger, starting with a body length of three to four inches, allow it to rest on your shoulder for more extended periods of time (e.g. 30 minutes while you are working at a table or watching television).
Care: House in large cages or chameleon trees. Basking site temperature 86-90°F (31-32C). Because veiled chameleons grow quickly, they are very susceptible to metabolic bone disease and care should be given to supplement their diet with calcium and vitamin D3, taking care to reduce the amount of vitamin D3 if they have access to a UV-B source. Veileds have a propensity for feeding on plant matter. Once a veiled chameleon has a snout to vent length of about three inches, skip feeding insects one out of every two or three days. If allowed to get hungry, your veiled chameleon will start nibbling on vegetation. Feeding insects every other day and alternating with dishes of plant matter such as romaine, kale, hibiscus flowers, kiwi fruit and grape sections will reduce the fat content of the diet and will help your veiled chameleon live longer.

An adult male veiled (*Chamaeleo calyptratus*) chameleon is easily recognized not only by the high casque but also by the brighter color, hemipenal bulge and tarsal spurs.

MEDICAL PROBLEMS

It is a good idea to investigate who in your area is a good reptile veterinarian or more specifically, a good chameleon veterinarian before you actually need the services of such a vet. Consult with local herpetological societies. Veterinarians inexperienced with chameleons will often do more harm than good and cost you a great deal of money while failing to treat your chameleon properly. Good chameleon veterinarians are rare but will be honest about the prospects of treating a chameleon and often enough may end up saving a chameleon's life. Basic fecal exams and parasite checks can be performed by most veterinarians but any advice about treatment should be based on literature by experienced reptile vets (such as Drs. Tom Boyer, Roger Klingenberg, Scott Stahl, and others). Whatever the case, isolate sick chameleons in a room other than one housing other chameleons. Prevention through quarantine of new animals and high quality care is highly recommended.

The following is a very brief overview of some of the most common medical problems encountered with captive chameleons.

Dehydration
Signs: Skin forming fine crinkly wrinkles, and appears dry; sunken eyes; listlessness; weakness; weight loss.

Treatment: If chameleon is still relatively active and alert, offer water or Pedialyte® several times a day. With animals too weak to drink on their own, a qualified veterinarian should be consulted.

Metabolic bone disease
Signs: Shaky and jittery when moving or episodic tremors followed by bowed limbs; spinal deformities; bent casque; soft lower jaw; inability to feed; inability to use tongue properly or to chew; listlessness; lack of appetite.

Causes: Lack of calcium or, if animal is receiving calcium, calcium is unavailable to the animals system due to other contributing factors such as lack of vitamin D3 or UV-B light source, inadequate heat, inadequate vitamin supplementation, incorrect calcium/phosphorus ratio, etc.

Treatment: Supplement diet with a calcium/vitamin D3 supplement. Allow exposure to unfiltered sunlight (always provide shade and NEVER use a glass or plastic aquarium) or artificial UV-B source. Provide adequate heat. In cases where an animal is weak, inactive, and unwilling to feed on its own, consult a veterinarian.

Vitamin A deficiency

Signs: Blepharitis (puffy eyes); eye weeping and crusting; problems shedding; inability to effectively use tongue; infections of sinuses (unilateral or bilateral small pea-shaped lumps on top of rostrum); respiratory symptoms; star gazing; and stiff, slow gait in severe cases).

Treatment: Depending on severity of symptoms, either treat by providing regular supplementation with a vitamin/mineral product containing some formed vitamin A. Feed insects grated carrots, cooked yam and foods with beta-carotene. In severe cases, consult a qualified veterinarian experienced with chameleons.

Neck/throat/upper chest edema (swelling)

Signs: Collar-like swelling of neck, or localized swelling of throat or lump-like swelling of upper chest.

Causes: These edemas may be caused by different diseases. One common interpretation is that hypervitaminosis (excessive) A or D are the cause of collar like neck edemas but they are not necessarily the cause of throat or upper chest edemas. Another suspected cause is hypothyroidism or hyperthyroidism. Because neck/throat edemas in certain species of anole have been successfully treated as signs of hypothyroidism, this requires further investigation in chameleons. Temperature because it affects metabolic rate in reptiles also appears to play a significant role in these edemas.

Treatment: Until more is discovered on the causes of these edemas, treatment is speculative. As a rule avoid high D3 supplementation in animals exposed to sunlight and with small, slow growing and montane species of chameleons. Avoid excessive vitamin A supplementation particularly with small, slow growing and montane species. Provide a basking site where chameleons can achieve an optimal temperature.

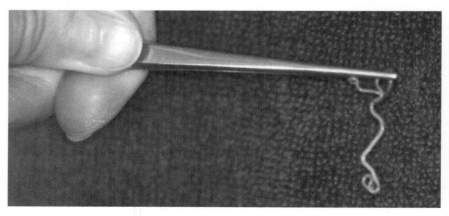

A filarial worm extracted from under the skin of a panther chameleon.

Parasites/Gi tract infections

Signs: Weight loss; runny stools; discolored stools; worms in stools; listlessness; weakness; sleepy; failure to feed (although some affected chameleons will eat a lot).

Treatment: Consult a qualified veterinarian for a fecal exam, diagnosis and treatment. Do not use ivermectin on adult imported chameleons prone to filarial worm infections.

Subcutaneous worms

Signs: Outline of worms under the skin. These are usually filarial worms. These worms are common in some Malagasy chameleon, particularly imported panther chameleons. They are also common in some groups of Senegal chameleons. Treatment: Make a tiny incision at the location of the worm and remove with fine tweezers. Swab with hydrogen peroxide. Small incisions will close quickly on their own. It is recommended that you consult a veterinarian if you cannot perform this, as cutting too deeply can cause additional problems. These worms will also be present as microfilaria in the blood stream. This stage is treatable with ivermectin in young animals but larger chameleons are best left untreated because of high risk of death.

Mouth infections

Signs of infection and swelling along the gum line, yellow caseous matter in mouth juncture, hard black "scabby" looking matter protruding from gumline in the front of the mouth, difficulty to feed or refusal to feed.

Treatment: Clean out the site of infection if caseous matter is easily removed. Apply topical antibiotic solution or ointment. Increase vitamin C in diet and generally make sure you provide adequate vitamin/mineral supplementation, as other deficiencies may be involved (vitamin A and calcium have been suggested). Some mouth infections have been known to heal solely with the daily use of additional powdered or liquid Vitamin C in the diet. Consult a veterinarian who will administer effective antibiotics if you have any doubt about dealing with the infection.

Tongue infection

Signs: Failure to fully extend tongue when feeding. Tongue appears swollen and/or gular area is distended. Failure to feed or use tongue altogether.

Treatment: Consult a qualified veterinarian who will administer an antibiotic.

Shedding problems

Signs: Failure to shed, flaky or excessive shedding (do not confuse with normal and frequent shedding of juveniles during growth).

Upper chest edema in a chameleon. The cause of this type of edema has not been clearly identified. More commonly edema around the neck area is seen and is believed to be caused by some type of hypervitaminosis, possibly combined with temperatures that are too low.

Causes: Illness and dehydration may prevent proper shedding. Too little or too much vitamin A or other vitamins can also cause shedding problems. You need to examine your husbandry methods and correct the problem. If your chameleon is sick you need to treat it.

Small white raised granular bumps on skin or dry scaly patches

Cause: Can be fungal or bacterial but in some species, like Jackson's and Meller's, it is often fungal. Overcrowding leading to small punctures in skin and excessive humidity are often associated with these signs. Isolate from other animals. Consult a veterinarian.

Swellings of limbs or extremities

In imported animals, swelling of limbs or extremities can be due to crushing trauma in the course of collection. Sometimes this goes away on its own, sometimes it is followed by secondary infections. This is also a possible sign of gout. If swelling increases rather than decreases consult a qualified veterinarian.

Hyperextension of the tongue

Signs: Following a strike, the tongue remains extended and fails to return to the mouth.

Treatment: Place your chameleon in a bare tank with a single low branch to hold onto, holding the animal and its tongue very carefully so as not to injure the tongue. Use moist paper toweling or wet news-paper to cover the bottom of the tank so that the tongue does not dry out or become stuck. **Never use a heat pad or under-tank heater!** To minimize stress and encourage muscular response, it may be helpful to place the tank in a comfortably warm (around 75°F) dark area. While this may look horrifying, a chameleon usually will withdraw its tongue within 24 hrs and return to full normal function without intervention. Refrain from jumping the gun and causing further irreparable damage. Calcium deficiency may be an associated cause.

Respiratory infections
Signs: Gaping and puffing with forced exhalations are usually signs of respiratory infections. This will often be accompanied by other signs such as keeping one eye closed or puffy eyes, inflated body, loss of appetite, failure to bask, and weakness.

Treatment: Keep the animal at its optimal temperature and consult a qualified veterinarian who may recommend treatment with an antibi-otic.

Note: Gaping and forced exhalations may also be signs of other dis-eases such as parasite infections.

Failure to lay/Egg binding
Signs: Egg outlines visible through sides, females weak, sunken eyes, tendency to stay at ground level but never performs effective nest dig-ging.

Treatment: Administer an easily absorbed calcium source such as cal-cium glubionate (Neocalglucon®) once or twice daily. Offer food or if female is too weak, a liquid diet such as Ensure® or a thin mix of Kaytee® baby bird hand-feeding formula. Be careful to prevent aspira-tion of liquid by the chameleon. One good way to do this is by filling a syringe with the formula to be used and slowly dripping it onto the front of the mouth until the animal begins to drink. Sometimes drinking can be initiated by getting a "taste" of the supplement into the mouth by pulling down the lip and placing a drop along the gum or by pulling gently on the gular skin and placing a single drop on the tongue. Never shoot it into the animal's mouth all at once. Another way to avoid aspi-ration is to insert a small syringe or feeding tube down the chameleon's esophagus. An experienced veterinarian can show you this technique. Also provide a suitable site for laying. After several days you may want to consult a qualified veterinarian. Egg-binding can be life-threatening and is more likely with overfed, dehydrated, ill or over-supplemented females. Do not confuse normal nest-seeking behavior with egg-bind-ing. Finding a suitable nest site can sometimes take days with the gravid female digging several test holes along the way.

WANT MORE INFORMATION ON CHAMELEONS?

Coming in winter of 1999 from the Herpetocultural Library!
The Chameleon Manual by Philippe de Vosjoli et al.

Available now. *Care and Breeding of Chameleons*, edited by Philippe de Vosjoli and Gary Ferguson, Ph. D. The Herpetocultural Library

Publication

The Vivarium magazine, the finest color publication in herpetoculture has articles on chameleons and related husbandry topics every issue. To subscribe call: 1-800-982-9410, 24 hours a day or go to www.thevivarium.com
Many articles on chameleons are also available through
www.thevivarium.com